Take Care of Yourself

Exercising

Siân Smith

www.raintreepublishers.co.uk
Visit our website to find out
more information about
Raintree books.

To order:
☎ Phone 0845 6044371
🖷 Fax +44 (0) 1865 312263
🖳 Email myorders@raintreepublishers.co.uk

Customers from outside the UK please telephone +44 1865 312262

Raintree is an imprint of Capstone Global Library Limited,
a company incorporated in England and Wales having
its registered office at 7 Pilgrim Street, London, EC4V 6LB–
Registered company number: 6695582

Edited by Dan Nunn, Rebecca Rissman,
  and John-Paul Wilkins
Designed by Victoria Allen
Picture research by Tracy Cummins
Production by Alison Parsons
Originated by Capstone Global Library Ltd
Printed and bound in China by Leo Paper Products Ltd

ISBN 978 1 406 24160 0
16 15 14 13 12
10 9 8 7 6 5 4 3 2 1

British Library Cataloguing in Publication Data
Smith, Siân.
Exercising. – (Take care of yourself)
613.7′1-dc22
A full catalogue record for this book is available from the
British Library.

Acknowledgements
We would like to thank the following for permission to
reproduce photographs: Capstone Publishers p. 23a; Corbis
pp. 4 © Christina Kennedy/DK Stock, 9 (© Kris Timken/
Blend Images); Getty Images pp. 8 (Photo and Co), 13
(ImagesBazaar), 19 (Jena Cumbo), 21 (Paul Debois);
istockphoto pp. 5 (© sonyae), 11, 22, 23c (© kali9), 16
(© Rhienna Cutler), 17 (© Alexander Semenov), 18 (©
Robert Dant), 20 (© Vladimir Nikitin); Shutterstock pp. 6 (©
CHRISTOPHE ROLLAND), 7 (© Morgan Lane Photography),
10 (© oliveromg), 12 (© Elena Elisseeva), 14, 23b (© Felix
Mizioznikov), 15 (© greenland).

Front cover photograph of smiling boy in swimming pool
reproduced with permission of istockphoto (© insagostudio).
Rear cover photograph of children stretching reproduced
with permission of istockphoto (© kali9).

Every effort has been made to contact copyright holders
of material reproduced in this book. Any omissions will be
rectified in subsequent printings if notice is given to the
publisher.

We would like to thank Nancy Harris and Dee Reid for their
assistance in the preparation of this book.

Contents

Exercise

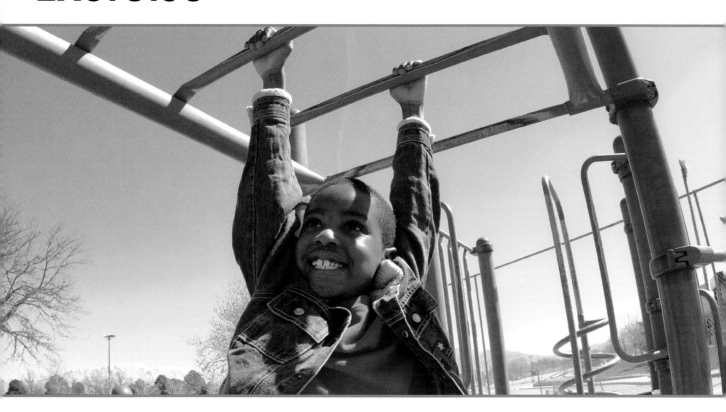

You need to do some exercise every day.

Exercise keeps your body healthy.

Every day

Do some exercise that makes you breathe fast every day.

You could play chasing games.

Do some exercise that makes your heart beat fast every day.

You could play sports.

You could skip fast.

If you can, stretch before and after you exercise.

Bones

Do some exercise that makes your bones strong.

You could hop or run.

Muscles

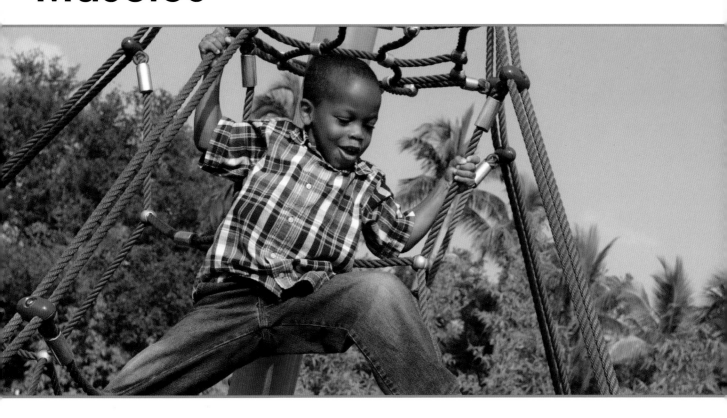

Do some exercise that makes
your muscles strong.

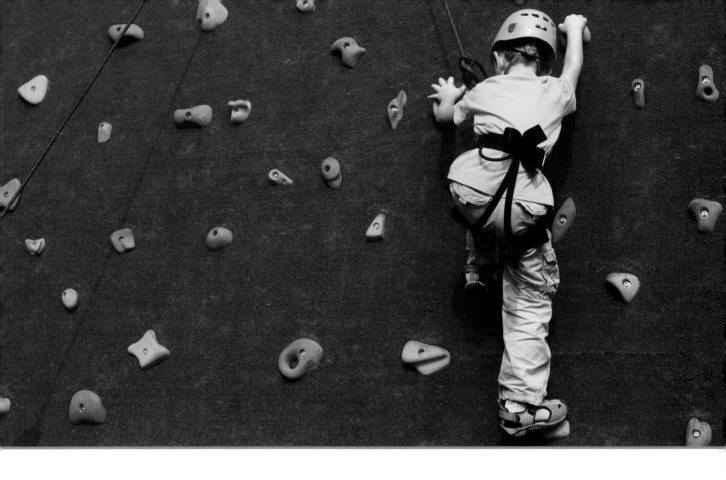

You could try climbing.

Gentle exercise

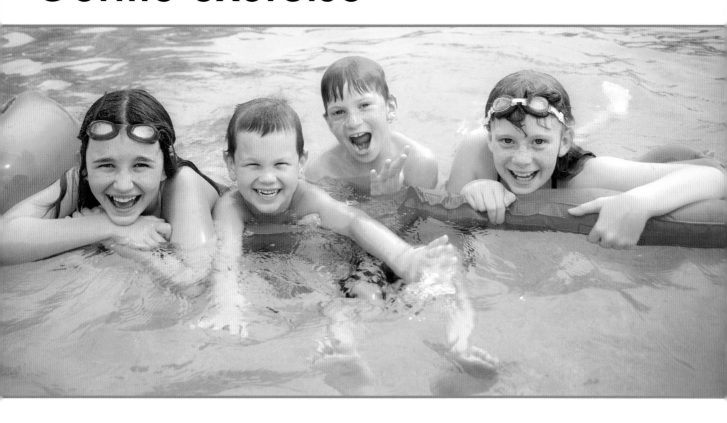

Gentle exercise helps your body, too.

Walk whenever you can.

You could ride on a scooter.

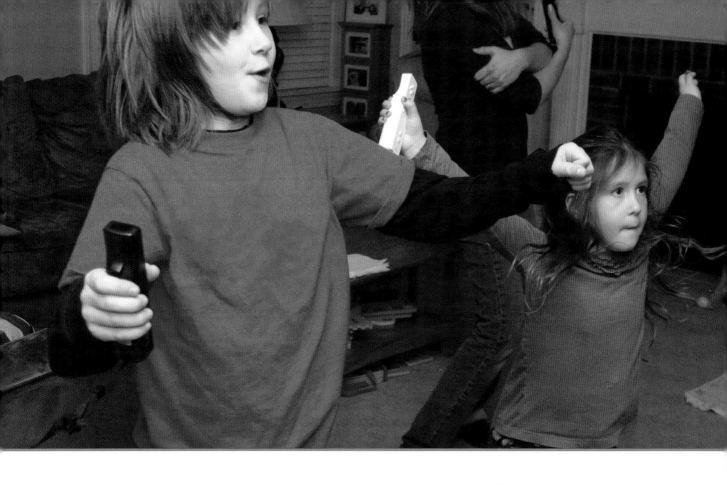

You can even exercise while
you play games.

Exercise makes your body strong
and helps you sleep.

Exercise can be fun!

Can you remember?

What should you try to do before and after you exercise?

Answer on page 24

Picture glossary

 bones you have bones inside your body. Bones help to keep your body up.

 muscles stretchy parts inside your body that can make things move

 stretch gently pull or push parts of your body

Index

Answer to question on page 22
You should try to stretch before and after exercise.

Notes for parents and teachers
Before reading
Ask the children why exercise is important. Explain that we need to exercise to keep our bodies healthy. Exercise strengthens our bodies and keeps our hearts, muscles, and bones working well. Exercise can even help us to improve our thinking skills and sleep better.

After reading
- Divide the children into pairs and give them time to think about their three favourite ways of exercising. This can include playground games, too. Ask each pair to share their ideas, then group the children into new pairs and ask them to share their ideas again. Did this help them to find other types of exercise that they want to try? If possible, try out some of these together.
- Investigate some of the benefits of exercise with the children. Try holding an early morning exercise session every day for a week. Remind the children of the importance of warming up and cooling down exercises during the session. Reflect upon any benefits the children feel as a result of the exercise and keep a class journal of these.